FOUR DIRECTIONS

FIRST EDITION, 2015

Four Directions
© 2015 by Joseph Bruchac

ISBN 978-0-9903204-7-0

Cover Art

Four Directions © 2015 by Whitney Luedtke

Author Photo by Eric Jenks

MONGREL EMPIRE PRESS
NORMAN, OK

ONLINE CATALOGUE: WWW.MONGRELEMPIRE.ORG

This publisher is a proud member of

[clmp]

COUNCIL OF LITERARY MAGAZINES & PRESSES
w w w . c l m p . o r g

Book Design: Mongrel Empire Press using iWork Pages

FOUR
DIRECTIONS

New and Recollected Poems

by

Joseph Bruchac

MONGREL EMPIRE PRESS
NORMAN, OKLAHOMA, UNITED STATES OF AMERICA

2015

My sincere thanks to the following places where earlier versions of some of these poems first appeared:

Blueline, "Mink"
Cream City Review, "The Cave at Quartz Mountain"
Groundswell, "Rough Sod"
High Rock Review, "The Bottle"
Long Island Quarterly, "We Are the Story"
North American Review, "Indian Country Again"
Spawning the Medicine River, "Corn Leaves"
The Tarascon Poetry Festival, "Four Directions"
The Arrow Finds Its Mark, "Just Listen to the Elders"

CONTENTS

In Flight	1
Four Directions	2
Just Listen to the Elders	5
We Are the Story	6
Everything Stops	7
Looking	8
Maskwa	9
Sun Moves	10
Swimming with Whales	11
Island	12
A Song for Bonsu	14
Current	16
Wind in November	17
Writing by Moonlight	18
The Bottle	19
South Branch	20
Deer Pond	21
Sweat Lodge by Bell Brook	22
Rough Sod	23
Azwa8zi	24
Little Wolf	25
Mink/Pottersville, NY	26
Glue	28
The Cave at Quartz Mountain	29
Photograph of Abenaki Boy and Bear,	30
Leaving Bristol, Vermont	31

Ogawinno   32

Corn Leaves in Italy   33

Flying Over Mount McKinley   35

Northern Lights at Midnight Near Chinook, Montana,
1989   37

Climbing   39

Tao Says   41

Indian Country Again   42

Memorial Guide   43

At the Vietnam Memorial   44

With Peacemaker's Eyes   46

Season's End   51

This book, inadequate as it may be, is dedicated to the memory of my wife, Carol.

IN FLIGHT

The temperature dipped
below forty last night.
Now, even though
late August heat
still ripples air over
the blackbird marsh,
the final turning
of this season's page
is less than a chapter away.

Out the window
past my offering
of sugar water
I see the roll
of southern slopes
soon to be whirred over
by hummingbird wings,
twin blurs of motion
as hard to see
as the thread
of spirit between us.

Though my own heart
is a thousand times slower
it beats in response
to the same painful bliss
of a summer's passing
the dying of light.

And, somehow, against all reason
our lives still remain together in flight.

FOUR DIRECTIONS

1.
Let us begin
by drawing a circle
that shape our ancestors knew
not as a symbol
but alive as the flow
of blood through our bodies
a cycle which sustains our lives

2.
When we humans
make circles
they are not perfect
sometimes the shapes
of our circles are broken
yet it takes only
one person's arrival
to make a circle complete

3.
Sometimes we see only
part of the circle
the way we see only
the arc of the sun
when a new day begins

4.
If we make a cross
within that circle
it does not stand
for a murdered god
it connects our center
to Mother Earth
to Father Sky
to our ancestors
and our children's children,
generations to come

5.
Place another circle
within each quadrant
Those circles remind us
of the seasons:
Spring with new life
like the gentle fawn,
Summer filled with light
like the eagle's wide wings,
Autumn when the Three Sisters
Corn, Beans, and Squash
give us their sweet blessing,
Winter, the strong time of rest,
like the Great Bear sleeping
in deep snow

6.
Those four circles also
stand for our Grandparents,
supporting us on every side
death does not take them from our lives

7.
When we bend that cross
it becomes the four winds
that circle our Earth
as lungs circle breath

8.
Now place this circle
on the back of Turtle
as our Earth was placed
when it was created
And when Earth moves
beneath our feet
we know Turtle is stretching
reminding us we are on that circle
and everything, every thing
is alive.

JUST LISTEN TO THE ELDERS

Words from an interview with Hastings Shade, Deputy Chief of the Cherokee Nation

There's no secret
to it,
just listen
to the elders.

Then they
look at you
they see you —

not just who
you are
but what
you are

just by
looking
at you.

There's no secret
to it,
just listen
to the elders.

WE ARE THE STORY
Native people believe
in what cannot be seen.

—Lincoln Tritt, Koyukon writer

Our elders, even when they talk
about themselves
sound as if they are speaking
about someone else.

The river is every
drop of water.

You're not part
of the tribe.
You are the tribe.

There is no past,
there is no future
there are only the voices
of our people
saying

that we
are the story.

EVERYTHING STOPS
Based on the words of an anonymous Dakota Elder, circa 1880

Everything, as it moves,
now and then stops.

The bird as it flies
stops in one place
to rest from flight
and in another
to make its nest.

And so, at times,
the Great Mystery stops.

The Sun, so bright and beautiful,
is one place where out Creator stopped,
as are the Moon, the Stars, the Winds,
the Trees, the Animals, and all of us.

So our people must stop
from time to time
to think of those places
and send our prayers.

LOOKING

Looking out the back window of a van going at 70
miles an hour down the back roads, heading towards
Tahlequah, the trees rushing away from us, the dark
roads behind growing ever smaller. A cigarette flicked
back from the driver is a sudden crescendo of sparks
and the shapes which pass are no more than pebbles
dropped into the dark waters of a lake, falling deeper
and out of sight.

Entering the heart of the Cherokee Nation, our faces
turned backwards, looking away from the lakes made
by government dams that drowned the small traditional
towns, looking away from Tsa-la-gi where the people
dressed as ancestors carry more weight of dream than
any tourist ever sees, looking back, back into old time,
looking into hills which are the true shapes of the hills
around us that are only shadows, looking back, listening,
hearing the voices, seeing the shapes of the Little People
who nod and watch us as we pass.

MASKWA

Scars on the trunk
of the white birch trees

shapes of the birds
whose wings open into thunder

marks
Sky Beings placed
on this tree
lightning never strikes

lift our eyes
beyond
the sound of guns

signs
that as we move
and keep moving
help us stay

SUN MOVES

Overhead
and I measure the day
by the span of my hands

I do not understand
minutes, hours, or time
except in the movement of light

Sun shares its warmth
but I cannot keep it,
cannot truly own anything
outside my skin

I do not understand
budgets, deficits,
dollars, defense, deterrence

Sun goes down behind hills
and the night reminds me
that darkness brings stories,
that rest is right.

I do not understand
the endless, frantic dance
of lighted screens

I understand sleep
I understand dreams

SWIMMING WITH WHALES

This water is theirs,
shaped by their fins,
yet they seem unconcerned
as my canoe
shares the tide.

They sweep by as slow
as the reflected motion
of cloud across sky.

Leaving the boat,
salt buoys me up
as their great bodies pass
close enough to touch.

Now, back on land,
I measure my passage
across earth we call owned
against their balance
in that place of no houses
where each current leads home.

ISLAND

I.

It was then
that the Manitou
said to the whale
as it lay in deepwater
its breath making waves
on each bank of the river
I can change you
into an island of stone

your body grey rock
your bones limestone
your eyes crystal
on your back moss and maples
and a thousand small bushes

you will not die
as the animals die
but wear slowly away
into waters
that love you

II.

I have seen it there
flukes of granite
sides silver ridges
of layered rock
eyes hidden under snow
eyes hidden under flowers
eyes hidden under brown grasses
eyes hidden under red leaves

I have seen it each time
I have ridden the train
that follows this water
foolish ones gave the name
of a man
and once
I saw it breathe

A Song for Bonsu
Ghana, West Africa, 1968

1.
In the cliff cut by waves
deep into the red cliff
below the fishing village.
the Gulf of Guinea rushes in,
leaves lacy foam at the edge of sand
clean and white as cloud
where rests a single bone
the length of a man.

It is the shrine of Osei Bonsu —
Chief Whale, the Fanti people say.
They know this ocean
is not their own and, long ago,
took up that bone washed to their shores.
With chants and drumming
they brought it here, a sign
from one who knows
greater depths than theirs.

2.
The songs the Fanti people sing
when in their small boats far from land
are those learned from the calls of whales,
music heard at night, remembered in dreams
when Chief Whale is a friend, a guardian.

3.
There are no shrines for any whale
here in our practical, western land.
The great rib bone that was left one night
by the storm which swept the beach at Keta
remains in Ghana, though I lifted it up
felt the thrill of power arced into its shape.

Yet, in this song, I return again
to that cave where humans still recognize
a kinship of spirit that goes beyond
the shores where most visions end.

CURRENT

The blue whales turn in the current.
Their ancestors were the same stars
that shape themselves above this night.

The sky is green, whirlwinds running
from horizon to horizon,
lifting the waves the way a grandmother
lifts the blanket from a sleeping child.

All of this, the warm ocean current,
the blue whales with their immense grace,
reflected by the shimmering green
of a dream before your face.

WIND IN NOVEMBER
Saranac Lake Inn, 1991

Wind Eagle greets me
as I speak its Indian name,
as I tell its tale
in this old hotel.

It rattles windows,
klon-gans against doors,
answers my words
in its own language,
its power turning
even human-made things
into instruments as easily
as its strums the branches of pines.

It will meet me tomorrow
in another state, its sweep
no less than this continent's breadth.
the span of its wings
touching every horizon,
bringing breath to every story.

Writing by Moonlight

Now the boat
floats still on the water,
the flow of the lake
slow as a sleeper's breath.

Wind blows from the west
towards the Great Bear.
The thin cry of the hunting bat
traces the line of a falling star.

The Night Sun
is the face of a drum,
The small stars
dance above the narrows.

The light on this page
is little brighter
than the shadowed fingers
that leave these dark circles and lines
that hold less of this night,
less of its song,
than my cupped hand holds
the lake and the moonlight
as I lift it
from rippling water.

THE BOTTLE

Walking through tall hemlocks
familiar to me as the lines
of a poem I once wrote,
I glanced down and saw
an old milk bottle
thrusting up
from the shine of needles.

As a boy, I might have sought a stone
to cascade that shape into bright shards.
Instead, I reached down,
took it into my hand.

Within it was a maidenhair fern,
green moss and light mist
formed from my hand's heat,
condensing drops of water beneath
the child's face of transparent white
etched into glass.

And I was wise or foolish enough
to take that bottle as a gift,
a message that however fragile
or empty the things we make might be,
given long enough, green may grow within them,
and decades spent close to the earth
can become filled with life.

SOUTH BRANCH
1948

My grandfather took me to that stream,
a continent of memory away.

The pine pollen drifting on its surface
pooled silver in sunshine under aspens
where old boulders eddied the water
into a shining, whispering circle.

Drop your line there, he said to me,
his hands opening to brush away
the pipe tobacco as he spoke.

And I dropped it, felt the electric shock
of the fierce, sudden, certain strike
as all of that stream transformed itself
into the twisting, alive, alive
body of my first brook trout.

DEER POND
1990

After a night in the city jail
my son Jim whistles to the loon
that dives and surfaces near our boat.

It's right, Jim says, after being set free
that we aren't catching fish today.

I smile back at him, remembering
how close the deer let him come
when we stopped on the logging road,
him walking slow in that old way
we were taught to return to sacred places
our old people lost when the timber barons
began to own land that owned itself before.

Spring rain comes walking across the pond,
comes washing away the smells of iron,
of concrete and urine and the feel
of steel wire mesh between fingers.

It always has been like this for us —
the way the old ways hold our hearts,
welcome our spirits back home.

SWEAT LODGE BY BELL BROOK

Crossing the stream
pooled waist-deep
behind piled rocks
lifting above the surface
like the knees of old men,
the bridge of boards
salvaged from the old shed
bends under my weight
but does not break.

Yellow jewelweed bobs
against my bare chest
painting orange pollen
across my skin
as I climb the hill
enter the clearing.

I kneel by the lodge
that still holds
the scent of sweetgrass.

The sand of ashes
from last night's sweat
spread like turkey's tail.

Pitted lava stones
from the southwest sit
in a quiet circle
around the fire pit,
elders waiting
for the council
to begin again.

ROUGH SOD

It peels away like skin as the spading fork
pries at the edge of the raspberry bed.
This green hair has roots, twining and pale
as the worms that fall free with each shake.
Dirt as dark as dried blood powders down
over raspberry corms, veins thrust through soil.

Transplanted, it will grow again,
fill in the space by the state road's edge
where the snow plows scoured too deep,
turn verdant once more that place where
the small, crowded blue spruce was lifted out.

By the brook, the last of that sod laid down
holds as a soft riprap, a cushion to kneel on
as I bend, leaning over the half-submerged stones
to wash the day's weariness from my hands.

Azwa8zi

Azwa8zi, have I grown weary
of the travails of this fickle world?

Like one of those 19th century poets,
lifting the back of his hand to his wan forehead?

No, that's not it.

I've just gotten bored
with their language of games

their unfailing ability
to fool themselves.

Azwa8zi, it is time
to change myself.

So I walk to the edge
of the furrowed field

I drive my tomahegan
deep into the ash tree

I hang my snowshoes there
and then

walk back into the forest,
become a bear again.

LITTLE WOLF

The eastern coyote, larger and bolder than its western cousins, is a hybrid animal, mixed since the early twentieth century with the remnant bands of timber wolves that survived in Canada's Algonquin Park.

Neither one nor the other,
a flow of blood between nations

you may find me still
within the woodlands

or if you have eyes for the night
see me walking among
their canyons of glass and steel
untroubled by the hum of wheels

Are you ready to cross the ice
of that river between

will you follow me

the toes of my unshod feet
splay out, sink down
into the snow
of the Starving Moon

as I drop to all fours
that sacred number
reaching down
through the white
to the brown earth
that holds us

MINK/POTTERSVILLE, NY
  1991

On the other side
of the potholed stream
mink makes its way
with smooth snake grace.
Small feet take
it from water to rock
into brush and then back again.
Sees us, smells us,
shows no fear.
Looks our way
with waterdark eyes
on the other side
of the flow where
rippled rock
and silver fish
fade into the lace
of current foam.

Its coat is dark, a night sky without stars.
Its teeth
whiter than cloud,
breath hot, quick
flicker of a small flame.
Yet, it is not hurried
as it makes its way
up and down the stream bank
then gone into ferns.

It leaves us watching
a long time, wondering,
at something
we might have been
four centuries or
an ocean ago when humans and animals
lived within stories,
eyes aware of each other
calm on opposite banks of the stream.

GLUE

The strongest glue, my grandfather said
was always made of horn and bone,
deerskin scraps ground down
then boiled thick and brown
as the sheen of a beetle's back.

Salvaged from the sacrifice of life
our four-legged relatives always gave,
that kind of glue held things together.

That was just how we did back in the day,
using everything the new people threw away.

THE CAVE AT QUARTZ MOUNTAIN
In Memory of Bill Stafford

Opened its one dark eye
beneath a ridge of smooth boulders,
old stones friendly to the touch,
holding sun's warmth through the night.

Under dry needled cedars, ripe currents.
One bush, arched like an eyebrow, hung
where a child might climb, dangle
one foot swinging as she picked the fruit.

In the midden corner, among chips of obsidian,
dark charcoal and glistening buffalo bone,
a Kiowa girl was unearthed by an archaeologist,
who recorded around her wrist a single bracelet.

And though, after eighty years in a museum,
her remains were finally returned to her people,
that bright beaded armlet was never found.

As I sat there that day, thinking of her,
resting away from the dazzle of sun,
a rustle of leaves, then a small ring-necked snake
out from under a stone, glistening red and black,
crawling over my arm and all around me was gone

lost with the smoke of our cooking fires,
the basket in which I placed the ripe berries,
yapping of camp dogs quarreling for scraps,
boys splashing in the river below our tall lodges. . .

this bracelet of memory cool on my wrist.

PHOTOGRAPH OF ABENAKI BOY AND BEAR,
Odanak, 1925, In memory of Atian Lolo, Stephen Laurent

The boy's hair is short, not hanging free
or long enough to tie to the root of a tree
and save him from being taken by witches.

Is that the reason he stands so close
and looks that way at the bear who is his friend?

The bear is young, limbs light with youth.
It has never known the sound of a gun.

Its eyes, perhaps, not yet old enough
to take in the box in which it stands
see the many ways the world around them
can cage a boy, can trap a bear
whose eyes look for the Dawn Land's light.

Did they walk together out of the frame?
Did they find a path they both could follow,
safe as the trails in the old days when
such brothers met and knew each other,
their prints the same in Ndakinna's soil?

LEAVING BRISTOL, VERMONT
1982

Two eagles circled
as I stopped by the road,
heading home from this town
where the old chief lies buried
side by side with whites in a cemetery
where his stone cannot be told from others,
names washed away by hilltop winds.
Their bodies did not resent his dark skin
joining theirs in earth.

Cedar needles, dried and brown,
fallen between the faceless fieldstones
from the trees that rose up,
green memories of the forest once here,
trees like those an Abenaki mother planted
at the head of her small son's grave
to sinew tall out of earth rich with life.

I held some of the cedar up to the sky
and the eagles circled,
turned their heads toward my eyes.

They watch this town,
ancestors not sleeping.

Holding the blessing of shared earth
they are keeping.

OGAWINNO

Ogawinno,
the sleeping person

My first place
is the one my eyes
opened to
when I began to dream.

Ogawinno

I knew no words then,
only the sound of my mother's heart,
the first touch of a warmth
that language can barely begin to reach.

Ogawinno

All of the world I would know was there
and it is still there, waiting for me.

Ogawinno

And just as pine needles pillow the earth
with decades of falling from an old tree's limbs,
the years between that first dream and this moment
have made a cushion for my feet and my mind to rest.

Ogawinno,
the respectful name
of the Bear.

CORN LEAVES IN ITALY
1976

Walking toward Lugano late at night,
it seems as if the entire world
has turned into highways,
smooth featureless houses
lining the macadamed shores.

Then, wire fence
cutting it off from the flow
of the midnight road,
a field of corn,
the last field of corn
in the world.

I jump the fence,
hold golden tassels
in my left hand
hand closest to my heart.

Maize, one of our Three Sisters,
strange to this land
as my grandfather's blood,
my divided feet,
yet somehow growing,
still growing.

I carefully pull
two leaves from a stalk.
And in my hands their scent
grows stronger as I
return to the roadside
where Black-eyed Susans
bob over the new concrete.

I kneel and bend
four blossoms together,
wrap the corn leaves around
to hold them together
as they hold me
from loneliness.

FLYING OVER MOUNT MCKINLEY
for Jim Weed

Denali, the Old One,
home of animal spirits,
your plume of snow
the feather of a chief,
the glaciers resting,
great beasts at your feet.

The news that day
all carried the story
about the climbers
lost on your face,
the storm closed
over their heads.

Perhaps, some said
as we passed above safely,
their eyes were closing
for the final time.

I whispered a prayer
for them and then
the clouds opened
as a plume of snow
blew across the southern ridge
where it rose above clouds,
a robe of seagull feathers
fluttering from a dancer's shoulders.

Clouds closed in again
after we passed.
But on the other side
in one open meadow
I saw moose grazing
where the tundra gave way
to the hopeful green
of that Arctic summer's
endless day.

NORTHERN LIGHTS AT MIDNIGHT NEAR CHINOOK, MONTANA, 1989

Two miles from Chinook,
just past Rock Creek,
two mule deer stood
eyes up toward a full moon
orange as a wild rose
above the sign marking the field
where Joseph's people
fought their final battle.

Still half awake,
half in a dream,
I kept on driving
across that prairie
between sandstone hills,
my heart seeing dark
until a shadow
turned into Coyote
crossing the road.

Tail straight out
like a streak of light,
he leaped and there
I saw to the north
the luminescent pulsing streams
of the Dancers at the Edge of the Sky.

That stopped me and
I stepped outside,
gazing up at the place high
above all claimed land,
my heart filled again
by a voice of spirit,
its presence bright as sky
painted with flowing light.

CLIMBING

1.

Climbing, climbing,
each time you reach
what you thought was the top,
there's more above.

2.

Deye mon, ge mon
beyond mountains, more mountains
they say in Haiti
where many peaks rise
above red, ruined land
and the forests are gone,
cut for cooking fires and tourist carvings.

3

It is said in India
that seeking God
is like climbing a mountain.
Each false summit shows
a greater height to come.

4

In one of our oldest Abenaki stories
Gluskonba was the one
who scaled Ktchi Wadjo
to bind the wings
of the great Wind Eagle,
then regretted his foolish deed.

5

So how does your tale
of ascending end?
Frozen forever like
the luckless on Everest
or Hemingway's leopard
on Mount Kilimanjaro?

Or if you do manage
to come back down,
what gift do you bring,
what hunger may greet you,
and to which side
will you return?

TAO SAYS

To lead the people
you must follow behind them.
When the leaders wear the finest clothes
the fields are filled with weeds.
The man who is brave and calm
will always preserve life.
Those who conquer
do so only when they yield.
Good men do not argue.
They know that the tree
which does not bend
will finally be broken.

INDIAN COUNTRY AGAIN
against Dick Cheney

It is time for soldiers to remember
the cemeteries of suicide angels,
carved heads tucked like robins
beneath their left wings.

Men as grave
as perched birds of prey
have bowed wise heads
that have grown grey
not so much from age
as from the falling decades
of battlefield dust.

They've reassured us we can trust
only what they've told to us.
They've learned a new way
to write words on the wind.

They have found
the Evil One's hiding place.
They have brought Custer's bugle
from its sacred case.

We shall make the distant deserts ours.
Great bouquets of smoke will billow up.
Black roses will cover the falling stars.

Let us sound the charge
against brown-skinned men.
It is time to ride
into Indian Country again.

MEMORIAL GUIDE

No one named Eagle
died in Vietnam,
according to this list.

There are two Bears.
But neither one, it seems,
was Native American.

Still there are more
than a dozen Hawks
and one is from
Indian Territory.

And while I'm looking
for Jim Bradshaw's name
on E17, Line 108
I find Thomas Lee Little Sun
born in Pawnee, Oklahoma.

His name in the dark
reflecting stone
shines like the light
of an unforgotten face.

AT THE VIETNAM MEMORIAL
   1983

A morning
hung with mist,
thick as that
which filled the delta
while from outside
the barbed wire perimeter
enemy voices called.
"Here I am, Joe."

Today you're here
and Joe is not.
His name is somewhere
on that black surface
which mirrors your face,
a partial survivor,
as you try to remember
the calendar day
that will show you where
on that long roll
your friend who died
is carved into stone.

Ching-ching, ching-ching,
a sound comes faintly
from the mist, out of the west.
Ching-ching, ching-ching,
as you look up
and the greyness opens
and you see three riders
come out of the fog
the way a dream
comes out of the night.
Ching-ching, ching ching,

the dancing bells
on their horses' fetlocks
beat out that old rhythm
which slows, then quiets
as they rein in.

Their faces are brown,
masked with yellow paint,
their long black hair
braided with ermine skins.
They wear bone beads
and eagle feathers
hang from their hair,
from the lances they carry
and from the barrel
of the AK-47
the man in back
holds up like a spear.

None of them speak.
The one in front
climbs slowly down,
to plant his lance
then turns, remounts.

Bells blend back into mist
living you alone
with the wind that blows
one healing feather
across your reflected face
and the name of your friend.

With Peacemaker's Eyes

More than a thousand years ago, when the Five Nations were locked in war, a man called the Peacemaker came to bring the people a new message of Peace for all from the Creator.

1.

We are watching
from within the longhouse
where our leaders are chosen
by the patient wisdom
of the gathered Clan Mothers
raised up by the will
and the love of all the people,
where the Eagle's wings answered
the songs of peace for the children,
the elders, the coming generations.

We are watching
as the Eagle watched
from the top of the great Pine Tree
buried over the weapons
of fraternal war.

2.

We are watching
from within the kiva
where the calm water in the seeing bowl
trembled and the picture formed
of distant events no longer distant.
broken arrows, steel winds of death,
black and burning rain.

3.

We are watching
from within the lodge
where the male deer remove their horns
so that even by accident
no one might be injured.
There, where the fire is held
in the glowing eyes of Grandfather Rock,
we sweat to purify ourselves
for all our relations
as we pray health and help
for all that lives

4.

We are watching
from the eagle-catching pit
without food or water or sleep
as Bear and Deer stand before us to speak
as Wind and Cloud take shape to whisper
as we see the far-off forms of greed
of hatred and hunger turn to spears of fire

5.

We are watching
from the shaking tent
from the Ghost Dance circle
from the Dreamer's lodge
from beside the Cross Fire
where Waterbird's wings
throb from the water drum

6.

We are watching
from Ndakinna,
from the Paha Sapa,
from beside the Sipapu,
from Cante Iste,
from the Big House
from the 7th Direction
from the Heart of the World
from that humbled place
within our own hearts
that only speaks
when we see ourselves
as Creation always sees us.

7.

We are watching
as the old Muskogee man watched
when the whirlwind approached him,
the great cyclone column
sweeping over the plain
toward his small house
till he raised the hatchet
in both his hands
to strike it down
into the willow stump
splitting the storm
to pass on either side.

We are watching
as the grandmother watched
the small silver screen
in her unheated trailer,
shaking her head in ancient pity

as the men in black judicial robes
sewed stones into their garments
and wading into the dark water
with its unknown depths
chanting hail to their chief.

8.

We are watching
as the white stone canoe
returns once more to the western shore.
We are watching as the calm Peacemaker
and Ayontwatha and the Mother of Nations
observe the approach of the Twisted Minds.

Earth shakes beneath their behemoth feet.
Their bodies are contorted by power.

Snakes grow from their hair,
the snakes of greed,
the snakes of hate,
the snakes of envy,
the snakes of deceit.

They hiss and coil,
those snakes of oil,
those snakes of blood diamonds,
those snakes of death squads,
those snakes of disease.

There is no force,
no human law,
no weapon of war
that can defeat those Twisted Minds.

Yet the Peacemaker and Ayontwatha
and the Mother of Nations are unmoved before them.
They wait in the cool shade of the Tree of Peace.
Behind them stand all of the people
who remember what Great Turtle taught them.
Hands joined together, they hear the drum
with its heartbeat rhythm begin to beat.
The Great Song of Peace will resound again.
Ayontwatha holds the bone comb in his hand.

SEASON'S END

This winter, the hardest one I've known
your heartbeat left this world.
The snow was deeper than dreams of sun,
it covered our windows, filled my throat.
The cold was strong enough to choke
all the words I thought I owned.

Late March has come, a new rain thrums
the canvas, makes the dark woods moist.
Mouths in marshes open in ancient chant.
My hands know it will not be long
before they spin the bow drill again.

The fire will glow, the lava stones
look at the world with eyes of flame.
Within the sweat lodge we will drum,
remembering we are promised nothing.
It is reason enough to join our voices,
my sons and I, for dead and living,
our breath reborn into song.

Author Photo by Eric Jenks

Joseph Bruchac lives in Greenfield Center, NY in the same house where he was raised by his grandparents. His grandmother Marion Dunham Bowman kept their house full of books and always encouraged him to read poetry. As a result, he was writing poems for his teachers by the time he was in second grade. He took his first poetry class while a sophomore at Cornell University, where he was the varsity heavyweight wrestler for three years.

At Cornell, Bruchac's poems were first published in the school literary magazine, *The Trojan Horse*, which he went on to edit. After graduating, he then got his Master's Degree at Syracuse University on a creative writing fellowship.

Married in 1964, he and his late wife Carol went to Ghana, West Africa for three years as volunteers, where he taught English. On returning to the USA in 1969, he and his wife founded an award-winning poetry magazine which they published for 18 years, *The Greenfield Review*.

Bruchac's poems have appeared in more than 700 magazine and anthologies and he is the author of over 30 books and chapbooks of his own poetry and editor of more than a dozen anthologies of poetry by other writers. His many honors include poetry fellowships from New York State and from the National Endowment for the Arts. A freelance writer and storyteller since 1981, he has also taught writing workshops in many schools on Indian reservations, and in prisons.

www.ingramcontent.com/pod-product-compliance
Lightning Source LLC
LaVergne TN
LVHW051607080426
835510LV00020B/3177